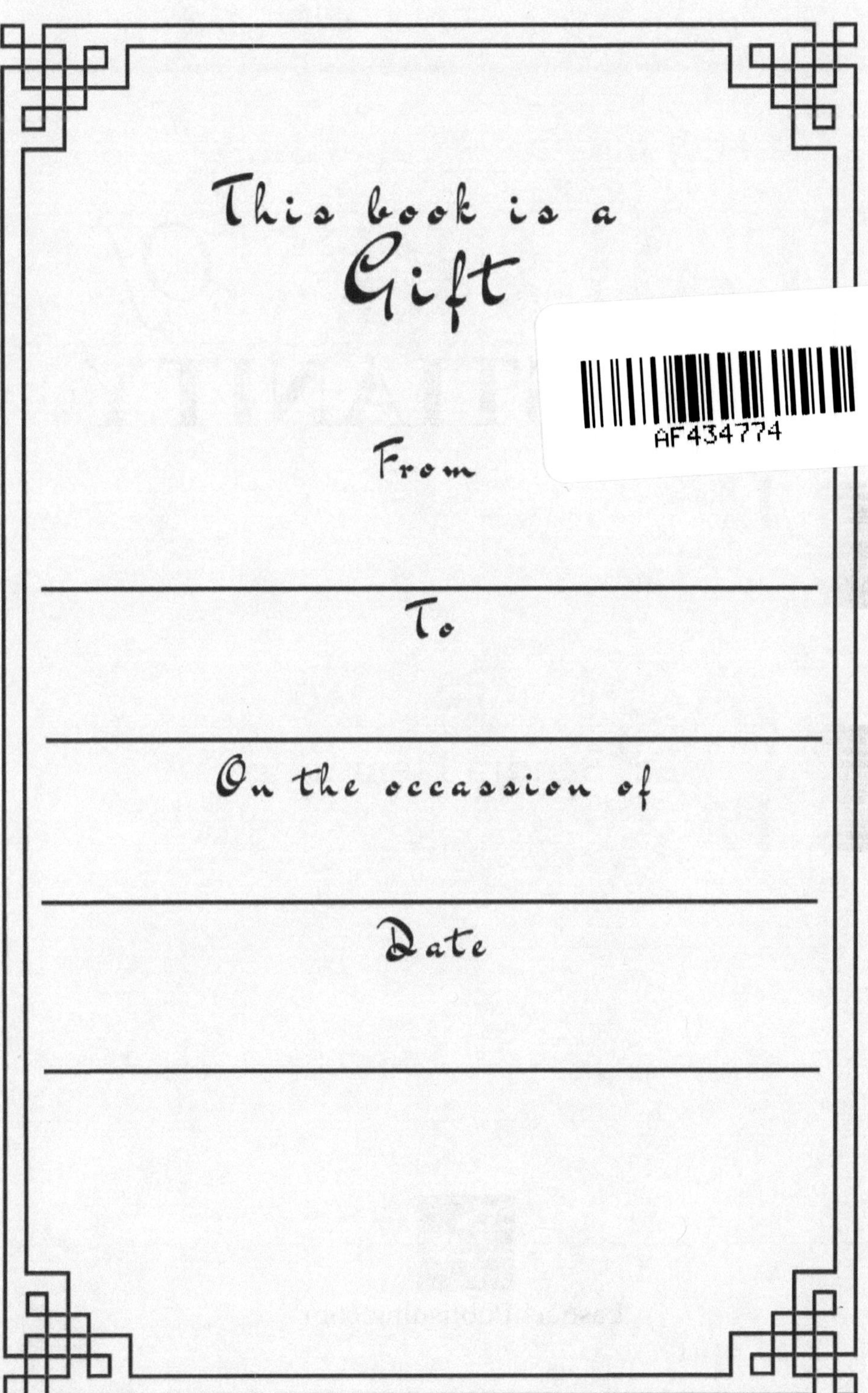
This book is a
Gift
From

To

On the occasion of

Date

FAILURES *Of* CHRISTIANITY

Dr. Sandra Flemming

LasouchPublishing.com

FAILURES OF CHRISTIANITY

Published by:

LASOUCH PUBLISHING: 11355 Richmond Ave, Houston TX, 77082, US.

+1 (917) 594-7014, +2348058092923

www.lasouchpublishing.com

ISBN-13: 9798747302556

Unless otherwise indicated, all Scripture quotations are taken from the King James Version of the Bible.

DEDICATION

To my three children

Esmond Flemming Jr

Tayib Flemming

Pastor Tebron Flemming

You are the best!

ACKNOWLEDGEMENTS

Pastor Esmond Flemming

Marigold Browne Dore

Dr. Melvorn Swanston

Amba Trott

Donace Caines

FOREWORD

All my life, I have listened to the gospel being presented by my mother, Dr. Sandra Flemming. She has always presented it in her captivating style which creates a hunger for more. Whether it was through the delivery of a sermon, drama or other, it was always well researched, informative and persuasive.

Failures of Christianity is no different. It comes with research, knowledge and is presented in style, yet it comes with much seriousness.

One cannot read and not reflect on the Great Commission of our Lord. One cannot read and not evaluate him/herself and the opportunities missed because of lack of awareness or indifference.

The question is yet to be answered: *"If we as Christians had been more like the Master commanded, would the world have been different?"*

Foreword

Pastor Tebron Flemming-Joseph
Pastoral @ Alpha and Omega Ministries.
Executive Director of Adult and Teen Challenge
St.Kitts and Nevis.

A SPECIAL WORD FROM THE AUTHOR

After years of waiting, God has chosen to release this book now as an ushering tool for the *End Time Harvest*.

We advise Christian-based institutions and organisations to ensure that a copy of this book is found on the desk of all leaders, ministers, pastors, Bible teachers, youth leaders and ministry departments.

- Teach church groups from this book.
- Expose all new converts to the contents.
- Bible colleges need this book. It is an important text book for today's Bible College.
- It's the best college graduation gift.
- Give it to your children as they leave your home to face the world.

A Special Word from the Author

Let us all be in this together as we win our world for our Lord and Saviour Jesus Christ. Amen!

Table of Contents

Table of Contents

13

CHAPTER ONE

The Introduction

01

> Tell your high priest to send one hundred skilled men in your religion and I'll be baptized and all my great men. You will have more Christians here than in all of the world.

Kubla Khan

CHAPTER ONE

THE INTRODUCTION

At an early age, I was so convinced that Christianity was right and the only right religion, I thought that everybody should become a Christian. In terms of major world religions, I did not know of any other religions then. Most of what I knew concerning false beliefs and practices were through songs: *"It won't be Harry Krishna or Rev. Moon."*

In 1989, I graduated with a diploma in ministerial studies from World Outreach Bible School where I learnt a lot. Among the courses taken was one on *"the Kingdom of the Cults"*. I was forever *"racing"* in my mind against such and became to whatever extent or degree, an apologist for that which I believed. I was so convinced that Christianity was right that I felt that it should be the only existing religion.

I also learnt about freedom of religion but I guess the argument was not as strong back then as it is now – with the penetration of our culture by non-Christian religions such as Hinduism.

In 1996 a book was given to me. In it was a story that I will never forget. It was so impacting that I wrote it out in my diary then and have transferred it from one diary to another several times now. I have also preached it to my congregations many times. It goes like this:

> In the year 1271, Marco Polo's father visited Kubla Khan, the great supreme ruler of China, India and the East. He had been so attracted to Christianity, that he said, *"Tell your high priest to send one hundred skilled men in your religion and I'll be baptized and all my great men. You will have more Christians here than in all of the world."* Nothing was done. Thirty years later a handful of men were sent. It was too few and too late.

Another story was documented in the same book:

> At the end of World War II, General Mc Arthur of Japan pleaded with the United States to send one thousand missionaries immediately. In one generation he said, *"Japan would be won to Christ"*.

Again the call went unheeded!

I saw them as tragedies and was convinced at that point that there were some major mishaps of Christianity. I never researched the mishaps but had seen and read enough. The mishaps are actually failures – **Failures of Christianity**.

Yes, there are some failures, some obvious failures of Christianity and that is what I expound on in this book.

S

CHAPTER TWO

Christianity

02

But ye are a chosen generation, a royal priesthood, an holy nation, a peculiar people; that ye should shew forth the praises of him who hath called you out of darkness into his marvellous light:

1 Peter 2:9

CHAPTER TWO

CHRISTIANITY

Christianity is by far the most outstanding of the major world religions. Other religions are founded on human figures and beliefs, while Christianity is founded on the life and teachings of Jesus Christ.

Being founded on Jesus Christ alone makes Christianity monotheistic: meaning we have and believe in but one God – the great God of the universe. There is none beside Him in all the earth. Surely, Christianity is the world's greatest religion and statistics also tell us that it has the largest following.

The word *"Christianity"* originated from an ancient Greek word *"Xpiotic"* which means *"Khristos or Christ"*, Christ meaning the anointed one. It is to this Christ we attribute the founding of so great a kingdom movement as Christianity.

Christianity began as a Jewish sect in the mid-first-century in what is now modern Israel and Palestine. It grew in size and influence for some decades and by the fourth century, it had become the dominant religion within the Roman Empire. During the middle ages, it grew under very challenging times. It has had its challenges and moments of apparent defeat but the great divine kingdom movement founded on the Only Begotten Son of God remains strong. It has never failed and it will never fail!

Christianity is now more than two thousand years old. Men and women, boys and girls, blacks and whites, Asians and Caucasians, the rich and the poor, the learned and the unlearned have come to Jesus Christ and have accepted Him as personal Lord and Savior and have joined His followers and have gone on to live a quality and standard of life that only Jesus Christ can give.

Christianity has approximately 2.2 billion adherents or followers and represents about one-quarter to one-third of the world's population. It is the state religion of our world.

Among all Christians, 35 percent live in the Americas; 25.7

percent live in Europe; 22.5 percent live in Africa; 13.1 percent live in Asia; 1.2 percent live in Oceana; and 0.9 percent live in the Middle East.

Followers of the religion of Christianity are called Christians. We were first called Christians at Antioch but before this, we were called *'People of The Way.'* Indeed we are the people of *'The Way'* because Christ Himself said *"I am The Way, The Truth and The Life; no man cometh unto the Father but by me."* This is what sets us apart; it is our distinction. We are different from the other religions and this is what makes us different.

Other religions look for other ways to the Father while we have found the way. The prophecy of Malachi the prophet in Chapter 3:1 reads that *"He shall prepare the way before me,"* and indeed he has. In the Word of God, people who had not found the way were described as wandering and lost. Christians do not wander. We have found the way.

James Emery White quoted Philip Yancey to be saying *"You can gauge the size of a ship that has passed out of sight by the huge wake it leaves behind."* Jesus' birth was so monumental that it split our reckoning of history into two parts: everything that happened on our planet – *"Before Christ"* and *"After Christ."*

Followers of Jesus Christ were first called a people of the way when it was first noted that there was a new movement in Jerusalem with a leader who was declaring the kingdom of God.

After being called a people of the way, we were first called Christians at Antioch, a city of Syria. We learn that the Latin suffix *'ian'* means *'belonging to the party of'* and was used to describe the followers of Christ. Warren Wiersbe says that it was out of derision that pagan citizens of Antioch joined the Latin suffix *'ian'* to Christ, hence Christian. It also meant little Christ or Christ-like – a derogatory statement. The name is found only three times in the New testament but nevertheless, we had been named as God planned: Acts 11:26, 26:28; 1 Peter 4:16.

Antioch holds other spiritual significance for us Christians. It was the home of the first Gentile church and it was also the haven of persecuted Christians.

Describing Christians

Who are Christians?

Christians are followers of Christ and Christianity is the kingdom movement that identifies us as His masterpiece, His chosen generation, His royal priesthood, His Holy Nation, who must show forth the praises of God who has called us out of darkness into His marvellous light. (See: Ephesians 2:10 [NLT], 1 Peter 2:9 [KJV]). We are the restored image of what He intended for us to be but was lost in the fall of man in the garden.

We are the people who uphold the teachings of Christ, who patterns our lifestyles and practices according to His teachings and practices. We describe ourselves as having been born again. We have had our sins washed away and now the Holy Spirit lives in our hearts and we are led by this same Spirit daily.

We are the people who were commissioned by Him in **The Great Commission:** *"Go ye into all the world and preach the Gospel, baptizing them in the name of the Father and of the Son and of the Holy Ghost; teaching them to observe all things even as I have commanded you."*

Warren Wiersbe in talking about Christians said *"Unfortunately the word Christian has lost a great deal of significance over the centuries and no longer means 'one who has turned away from sin, trusted Jesus Christ and received salvation by grace.'"* He said that many people who have never been born again consider themselves Christians simply because they say they are not pagans.

He cited and I agree wholeheartedly that belonging to a church or attending church services regularly or even giving to the work of the church does not make one a Christian. It takes repentance from sin and faith in Jesus Christ, who died for our sins on the cross and rose again to give us eternal life.

He referred to Dr. Otis Fuller who asked *"If you were arrested for being a Christian would there be enough evidence to convict you?"*

John Waddey, writing on first-century Christians wrote, *"Tragically, much of what is called Christianity today has little resemblance to that which Jesus created."*

The Pilgrim's Progress, a classic of the nineteenth century, written by John Bunyan describes the Christian as God gave him in a vision. He describes the Christian as the called out one who leaves his country and is headed for the celestial city. Sure, he met with perils, despondency and lions along the way but faith and hope were with him as yonder light burned bright. Yes, he made it to the celestial city!

CHAPTER THREE

First-Century Christians

03

> Jesus died and bodily rose from the tomb with full proof of His resurrection, and as promised, the Holy Spirit came in the New Testament book of Acts, chapter 2, equipping and anointing them, as they waited in the upper room

Dr. Sandra Flemming

CHAPTER THREE

FIRST-CENTURY CHRISTIANS

First-century Christians are the followers of Christ who lived between the period starting at the birth of John the Baptist and the death of John on the Isle of Patmos in about AD 100. Significant happenings during this period include:

- The birth of Jesus;
- The death of Herod who killed John the Baptist in about 4 BC;
- Control by the Roman Government;
- The onset of Jesus' ministry;
- The coming of the Holy Spirit at Pentecost, His actions throughout the book of Acts which initiates

the conversion of Paul the Apostle and his missionary journeys;

- The death of James, John's brother; and
- The writing of the gospels and epistle letters.

According to some scholars Jesus was born about 3 AD, others say between 4 AD and 8 AD and lived for about 33½ years. For the last three years of His life on earth, He took the public stage doing great miracles and training the twelve men who were with Him, who were called His disciples. He trained them, mentored them and equipped them for the taking of the mantle that He was going to pass on to them in a very short time.

He died and bodily rose from the tomb with full proof of His resurrection, and as promised, the Holy Spirit came in the New Testament book of Acts, chapter 2, equipping and anointing them, as they waited in the upper room, to carry out the task of the great commission as Jesus asked them to.

Legendary among His disciples, who were later called apostles, was one Paul, who though he was not one of the original twelve and as he claimed never saw Christ with his physical eyes, was instrumental in planting a number of the New Testament churches.

Paul was brilliant. He was strategic and used these characteristics positively in the development of Christianity after having used them negatively in the persecution of the church. He acknowledged Jesus as Lord after having a personal encounter on the Damascus road en route to securing written permission to persecute the church.

Paul's contribution spans more than thirty years and involved three missionary journeys and numerous trips and letters to the churches. Paul's further contribution was the laying on of hands and impartation for those who would assume leadership roles in the church as he moved on, oftentimes to church plant again. Those raised were called pastors. They were accountable to the apostles. Letters were written to counteract problems, encourage, and teach.

A significant contribution to the growth and development of the church also came from James – the head of the Jerusalem church. James was the Lord's brother and a skeptic during his earthly life.

Small groups soon began to spring up as the followers began to meet in groups, meeting needs, mentoring and raising others, and getting the gospel out as Jesus asked. They stayed in communities and encouraged each other while using the ability, wisdom, and strength that comes from the anointing of the Holy Spirit. These groups were like family and soon became churches.

The apostles laid hands on the leaders or elders in the spirit of impartation, setting them apart to lead and guide, while the apostles moved on to perform the same duties in another community. The leaders raised were or became the pastors.

Letters were written to counteract problems faced and to teach and encourage and remind. The letters are now parts of the New Testament. They were written to the different church groups. Paul was the main source for this type of exposure and accomplished greater, by far, than most of the other apostles.

The apostles travelled quite a bit, to meet for council meetings, prayer, and encouragement.

Christianity grew. It spread, and it crossed borders. From the book of Acts, we learn that from Jerusalem it spread to other places such as Samaria, Antioch, Iconium, Thessalonica, Athens, and elsewhere. Wherever the disciples went, Christianity took root. The disciples paid terrible prices with their lives. They were tortured, imprisoned, and martyred but the purpose God intended was realized. Christianity grew and spread. By AD 100 all the apostles had died. The disciples who had graduated to apostleship had practised and perfected the great commission as Jesus said.

First-century theologians were bishops and other ministers. They were leaders of congregations in the Roman Empire. These men were not apostles themselves but may have known one or more of the apostles.

CHAPTER FOUR

Dropping the Baton

> One of the earliest causes of corruption was the attempt to translate the Christian kingdom of God into a visible monarchy where the saints inherit the earth in a literal way.

Dr. Sandra Flemming

CHAPTER FOUR

DROPPING THE BATON

John was the last of Jesus' disciples or apostles to die. With his death came the death of the apostolic period. With the death of the apostolic period, the Baton was dropped.

Most of us are familiar with the dropped baton experience. In the heat of the moment of the race ... the winning or leading athlete drops the Baton; the alarms are raised, as we hear the ooh's and aah's of disappointment expressed. Just so it is with Christianity.

After all of the work done by Paul and the apostles in New Testament time (in particular the book of Acts where churches were planted and souls were saved and added to the church daily), we moved into an era called the *"Dark Ages"* where there was no longer obvious action of the Holy Spirit. There was only the Roman Catholic church and at that particular time, it was not led by men who were led by the Holy Spirit.

The Baton Was Dropped.

According to the book of Acts, Christianity had begun with just a small number of about one hundred and twenty followers but was seen as a threat to the Roman Empire as they refused to worship Roman gods and emperors. This led to persecution and martyrdom. This persecution ended under Emperor Constance (AD 285-AD 337) and the Romans legalized Christianity.

Constance, The Great proclaimed himself as the emperor of the people since he had become a Christian. Christianity then became the official religion of the Roman Empire instead of the old Roman religion which involved the worship of many gods.

The next generation of leaders was Polycarp, Ignatius, and Clement. These men followed in the steps of the apostles doing the same things. Polycarp had been personally tutored by John and was considered a personal link with and to the apostles. He himself, had disciples. He tutored and trained one by the name of Irenaeus.

Their contribution is invaluable since it was no easy task fighting heresies and sects that arose in the church. Following these men were about fifteen centuries of *"the dropped baton"* as I call it.

Justo Gonzales said that one senses a distance between the Christianity of the New Testament, especially that of Paul and that of the Apostolic Fathers.

Men of the second and third centuries such as Tertullian and Origen must be commended. They, too, combatted heresies such as Gnosticism, Celcius and Montanism and made every effort to keep the church pure.

Corruptions of Christianity

Corruptions of Christianity included Judaism; Roman practices and beliefs; Gnosticism, Celcius and Montanism, Immorality with immoral pietism; pagan superstition, and pagan philosophy.

One of the earliest causes of corruption was the attempt to translate the Christian kingdom of God into a visible monarchy where the saints inherit the earth in a literal way. The temptation was severe during the decay of the Roman Empire when civil authority became very weak and the real ruler was the principal clergy of the day.

This led to the bishops dressing as Roman provincial rulers. The impression was given that Rome had been abandoned by her emperors and that the chief citizen of Rome was the bishop. This corrupted Christianity because it led to the belief that Christ's kingdom was earthly — a visible monarchy.

It translated spiritual forces into physical and mechanical equivalents. The very term *'physical'* that belonged to the affections and emotions, thoughts, and will of the whole inward life was used to denote whatever belonged to the church and clergy.

Land — the writer, said it became spiritual when it passed into the hands of the bishops. Men were spiritual if they were servants of the church. Things were spiritual if they were church property. The sacred was forgotten in the strife for the world's position, power, and wealth. It went further because worldly men who went into the ministry were tempted to favour superstitious errors that brought profit and power.

People were led to believe that the priests can serve God in their stead and that there were mysteries in religion that only the priest could understand. Hence they followed blindly the guidance of the priest.

Christianity was also used by some rulers to oppress. Some were tyrannical rulers. It bred false views of Christian unity since it subdivided their neighbours under the propagation of their true faith.

Some were led to believe that they were not true Christians unless they belonged to one community that is visible and universal. This idea intensified other errors. People were convinced that they were to belong to one community on earth and dreaded the separation.

The Growth of the Episcopal

By the time of the fifth and sixth centuries, the government was episcopal. The principles on which it rested were now very different to the government of the Christian community in apostolic times.

The episcopate or clergy of bishops had become the form of government in about AD 70 and this led to the ruin of Christianity. AD 70 was the big turning point in Christianity. John, the last disciple was the only one alive when Jerusalem was destroyed and the church shaken. According to several scholars, it was at this time that the episcopate took the place of the apostolate and preserved the church. They prevented the church from breaking up into several small sects since there were no apostles and the New Testament canon was not yet a reality. It was at this time that the bishops rose and portrayed themselves as superior.

Their duties, however, seemed different to that of the Episcopal times. They laid claims to powers of rule over the

Christian community, not as chosen representatives of the Christian people, but as the official representatives of the apostles.

People's lives were dominated from birth to death by the Catholic Church. Christianity was the only recognized religion in the form of the Catholic religion. Whether peasants, nobles, lords, or kings, people's lives were dedicated to the church.

The church was powerful. It had its laws and lands and even imposed taxes on the people. It also took special gifts from people who wanted special favours or a place in heaven. The church was also very wealthy and with its wealth, its power grew. It influenced the kings and rulers of Europe.

Opposition to this great church, though far from God's intention and the apostolic age, resulted in excommunication. Excommunication meant that a person could not attend services, could not take sacraments, and would go straight to hell when he died.

Pagan Immorality in the Church

To ancient pagan thinkers and philosophers, the key to the hidden secret of the origin and preservation of the universe was in the mystery of sex. They taught that two energies or agents--one active or generative; the other feminine, passive or susceptible--were thought to combine to produce everything such as heaven, earth, sun, and moon. This led to polytheistic worship and prostitution became a solemn service and found its way into the church.

The struggle and fights of those years because of the misrepresentation of the church and Christianity caused the church to decline. It was an absolute far cry from Christianity and what it was destined to be.

After all of the accomplishments of New Testament time, the baton was dropped.

CHAPTER FIVE

Picking Up the Baton

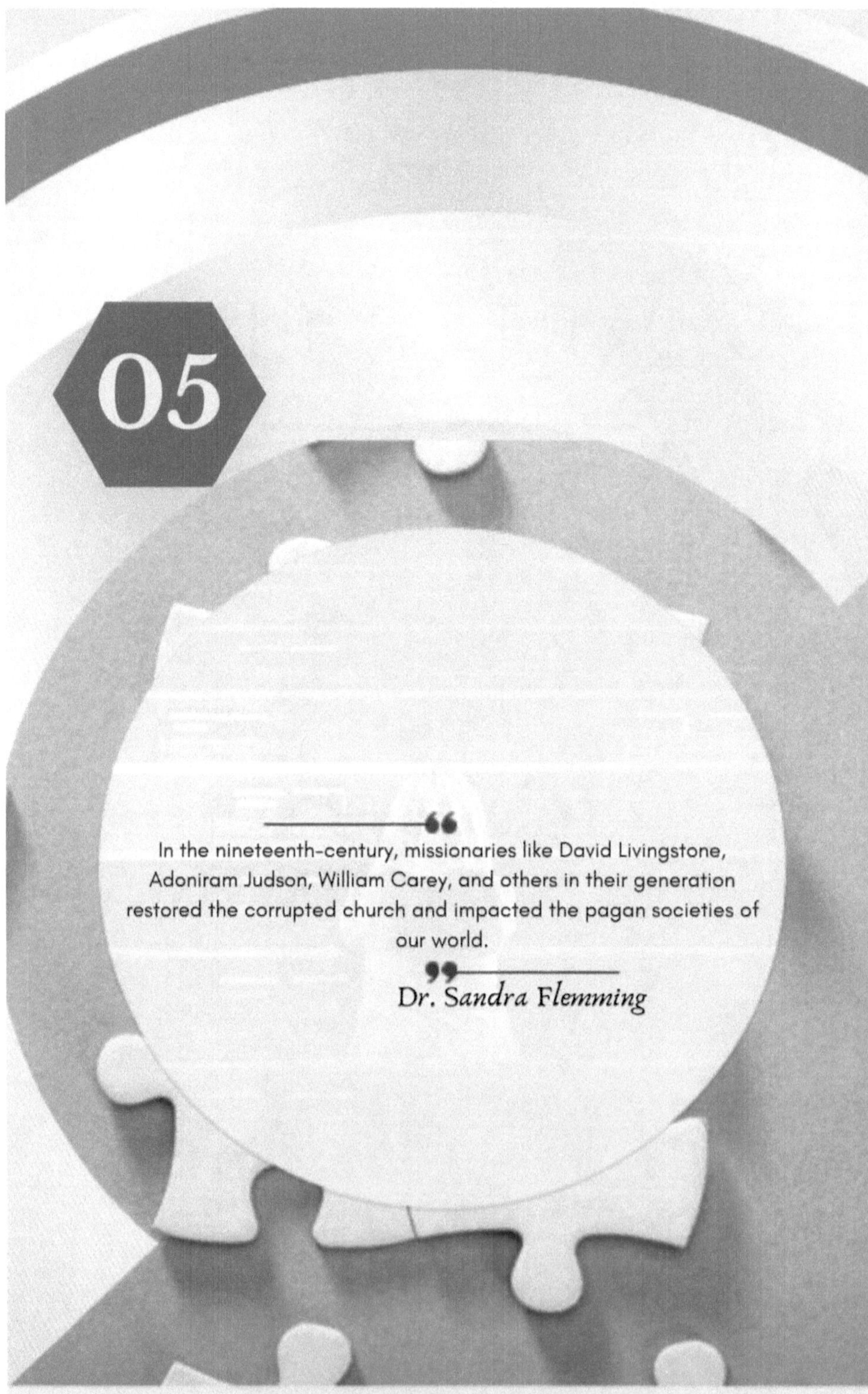

05

In the nineteenth-century, missionaries like David Livingstone, Adoniram Judson, William Carey, and others in their generation restored the corrupted church and impacted the pagan societies of our world.

Dr. Sandra Flemming

CHAPTER FIVE

PICKING-UP THE BATON

The Baton of Christianity was picked up with the initiation of the Protestant Reformation. After sixteen centuries of alienation from the Apostolic Age, Martin Luther *"troubled"* the church and brought us back to what Christ intended for His people. With him was John Calvin and other Protestants.

I was taught that Martin Luther, a German, wished by his father to be a lawyer had become a monk and lived in the monastery. He, one day while walking, discovered a part of the New Testament, the book of Romans. From his reading, he discovered that he, like all the rest, had been misled by the church – the Roman Catholic Church.

Subsequently in 1517, he wrote ninety-five theses and pinned them to the door of the church. These debated and criticized the church and the Pope but concentrated on the selling of indulgences and doctrinal policies about purgatory, particular judgment, devotion to Mary, the intercession of devotion to the saints, most of the sacraments, etc.

He also objected to the doctrines, rituals, and ecclesiastical structure of the Roman Catholic Church. Also, there were three men at that time claiming to be the Pope simultaneously. This eroded people's faith in the church and the papacy which governed it. The corruption of the system included false doctrines and malpractice by clergy and abuses of the people. The theses were nailed on the power and efficacy of the indulgences in the church.

The corruption of the system included false doctrines and malpractice by clergy and abuses of the people. Martin was excommunicated from the church because of his intervention. The date was January 3rd, 1521. This led to the creation of the Protestant churches.

I must number this among the failures. After all this great achievement, the reformers disagreed among themselves over doctrinal differences. First, between Luther and Zwingli and then between Luther and John Calvin. This consequently led to the establishment of different but, not only different, rival churches.

Worse yet, the reformers and their disagreement accelerated the development of the counter-reformation by the Catholic Church.

Ulrich Zwingli began a movement in Switzerland. He and Luther agreed on some issues, but disagreement because of unresolved issues separated them.

Other groups broke away from both Rome and Protestantism because of Mysticism and Humanism.

Picking Up a Baton

A public apology…

On August 28, 2009, the Southern Baptist issued an apology for its earlier stance on slavery. The issue had split the church between North and South in 1845. The apology came a century and a half later in 1995. It was also an apology for racism because the stance was for slavery and segregation.

One of the tragedies that affected the Christian Church relates to the Baptist Church and other churches and the stance they took on slavery, a stance in favour of slavery.

Read the following.

Baptist, Congregationalist, the Free Church, and slavery. An address delivered in Belfast, Ireland on December 23rd, 1845. Belfast Newsletter, December 26th, 1845 and Belfast northern Whig December 25th, 1845. Speech by Mr. Frederick Douglass: highlights from his speech...

Mr. Douglass stated that he did not want to be viewed as an enemy of the church. His duty, he said, was, as called upon, to expose the corruption and sinful position of the American churches with regards to slavery.

He said that he had not supposed that they would have descended to the low and mean act of upholding and sustaining a system by which three million people have been dehumanized instead of being given every right and privilege which they ought to enjoy. He said that unless the deeds of these ministers were made known, unless the light should be permitted to shine in the dark recesses, there will forever be a sink of iniquity in the midst of them. He said the only way of purifying our church from the deep damnation into which, the church was plunging was to expose her deeds to the light.

He said *"Let no man rank me among the enemies of the church or religion because I dare to remove the mask from her face and give the nations of the earth a peep at her enormities. It is for her own salvation and purification that I do it and for the redemption and enthrallment of my race"*.

He said that some persons took an offence to his saying that slave owners become worst after conversion, and thought that by making the statement, he was somehow injuring the cause of religion. He said that was the same principle upon which Christ denied the scribes and Pharisees when He said that they would compass sea and land to make one proselyte and after they had made him, he was ten times the child of hell than he was before.

He said The Baptist Church was congregational in its organization and government. He said that the congregations were united by a triennial convention. The object of which is to spread the gospel among the heathen. He said that the president of the convention was a slave owner himself. He is a man stealer. The secretary of the convention was another man stealer and most of the other officers were men stealers.

He said one man among them (now dead) was an abolitionist. The man, Elon Galusha, he said dared to say that a slave was a man and that slavery ought to be abolished. For this, the members of the church cast him out. A Rev. Lucius Bowles congratulated his brethren that there was a pleasing degree of unity among the Baptist throughout the land for the Southern Brethren were all slaveholders.

Mr. Douglass said that the slave owner was not to be ranked as a common criminal, as no worse than a sheep stealer or a horse stealer. The slave owner is not only practising thievery of men but he is a murderer, not a murderer of body but of soul.

He referred to an American paper with an ad by the legal representative of a Baptist minister, Rev. Dr. Furman – an eminent Baptist minister who said the scriptures warranted the holding of slaves. He said that the people should be weeping because a doctor of divinity had published this.

The Same Issue As It Happened In Virginia

In Virginia, the people regularly entered into the raising and breeding of slaves as a business much like the cattle business. There they would separate two slaves, male and female already married. When the Baptist society was asked if the separated could marry again, the answer was that the separation tantamounted to the civil death of both parties and that they were not forbidden to marry again in either case.

Mr. Douglass said that this was a deliberate setting aside of the marriage institution and the deliberate sanction of a wholesale system of adultery and Concubinage. He said that the persons who authorized and enforced such wickedness called themselves Christians.

Mr. Douglass said that there were facts after facts relative to the doings of Christian slave owners in America. He said the most ardent friends of the slave trade were the ministers. – the higher up the hierarchy we go, the colder the ministers in the cause of freedom. The leading doctors of Divinity in America and the professors in the colleges were in favour of slavery.

He referred to Professor Stewart of the Andover Seminary, one of the first Biblical schools of New England. He had committed to him the instruction of the ministers of a large portion of the congregational denominations and he was an advocate of slavery.

He referred to a Dr. Fisk who had been welcomed by the Methodist Church though they had shut him out. He had become uneasy when he heard it mentioned that slavery was a sin and was not willing to commit himself to the question. He wished to have the opinion of Dr. Stewart on the subject. He, Mr. Douglass said that this man who would have said that sheep stealing was a sin and would have decided so at once had to consult a learned doctor as to whether man stealing was a sin.

Dr. Stewart sent him a reply in which he referred to Onesimus whom he stated Paul had sent back to Philemon for life. Mr. Douglass, giving the speech said that there was no such thing as Jewish slavery for life. Paul, he said told Philemon to receive Onesimus as he would Paul, not as a slave, but as a brother.

Dr. Douglas must be commended for this bold, timely, and crucial initiative. I am sure others took his stance but he was the one who came to the fore at this particular time. He must be commended.

He exposed the deeds of the church as it relates to that particular issue, the issue of slavery and being slave owners. Beautifully and with distinction, he dealt with the failure that preceded him. This correction done on the public stage of the world surely would have impacted positively, not only his denomination but Christianity by extension. For Christ Himself said what is done in the dark must be brought to the light and it is in the light that confrontation is had. It was a victory for the church and Christianity.

Dr. Douglass denomination is strong: It is global in its presence and thrust.

Before this Period, Paul had a good understanding of the matter, he admonished Philemon a slave owner of the New Testament who had been converted during the time he was a slave owner to receive Onesimus as a brother and not as a slave.

Onesimus had been owned by Philemon but ran away having stolen from his master. It was on his run that he met Paul and was converted to Christianity. Paul was now sending him back to Philemon.

Christians do not practice slavery nor any derivatives of such. We have heard often that at the foot of the Cross, we are ALL equal.

Martin Luther

In the dark ages, church and state became one. The Roman Catholic Church dominated the lives of the people. The church was the authority of the day. Everybody was a part, through birth, marriage, death, etc. The passion for souls died because of this experience. It was a church filled with people without born-again experiences. Luther initiated change through his Reformation. John Calvin and Zwingli must also be mentioned here.

John Wesley

He too picked up the Baton and ran with it. In an effort to initiate change in the Anglican Church, he became a reject by the congregation but founded the Methodist Church where he proclaimed the doctrine of Holiness.

John Wesley was born on June 17th in the year 1703. He was very vocal about ordinary people being barred from the church. On many occasions, he was barred from the pulpit. It was because of these types of experiences he initiated field preaching, preaching to the people in open areas. He also preached from the marketplace.

Prior to being saved, as an Anglican minister, he travelled on a boat to Georgia to preach. While on the boat there was a storm and he feared for his life. On the boat also were some Moravians who were travelling to preach also. While Wesley feared for his life, they sang calmly.

After the trip, Wesley approached one of the leaders and asked about his serenity. The Moravian in turn asked him if he had faith in Christ. Wesley said he did but feared that they were vain words. He was confused by the experience. It led to soul searching and then, to his conversion.

In his words, he said, *"God in Scripture commands me according to my power to instruct the ignorant, reform the wicked and confirm the victorious, man forbids to do this…I have no parish of my own, nor probably ever shall. Whom then shall I hear God or man? I took upon the world as my parish, where ever I am. I judge it, meet it right and my duty is to declare unto all that are willing to hear, the glad tidings of salvation."*

From thenceforth he had nothing further to do with bishops. He built structures for the first Methodist churches that he started with his own hands. Wesley preached the word fearlessly and was a positive voice and force in the church, but alas the church did not always recognize it. He experienced a broken relationship that was used against him and was the subject of an untrue scandal. In his words, he said he had a conscious void of offence to God.

His brother, Charles in that same century wrote songs that spoke to the doctrines that had been lost in the Middle Ages. Charles wrote:

A charge to keep I have,
A God to glorify,
A never-dying soul to save
And fit it for the sky.
To serve the present age,
My calling to fulfil,
O may it all my powers engage,
To do my master's will.

In the nineteenth century, missionaries like David Livingstone, Adoniram Judson, William Carey, and others in their generation restored the corrupted church and impacted the pagan societies of our world. They made valid contributions in this era.

In 1678 John Bunyan wrote the Pilgrim's Progress.

In 1793 William Carey sailed for India.

These men not only had a dying soul to save. They heard and understood the call to serve their age, their generation and undoubtedly knew that they were responsible for the times in which they lived. They understood that they had a call to fulfil, the call to *'Go into all the world.'* They understood that with all their strength, intellectual abilities, and courage, God's Will was to take precedent over theirs and by their answering of the call.

Continents were brought from Spiritual darkness to light. It took sacrifices: many of them got diseases and illnesses that took their lives, the lives of their spouses, and the lives of their children but it was a calling to fulfil. They were never happy or fulfilled until they did what they were called to do or as the Word of God mandated.

CHAPTER SIX

Where We Are Today

> The tremendous tragedyof the twentieth-century evangelism can be summed up in two words 'No Fire'.
>
> *Robert L. Summer*

CHAPTER SIX

WHERE WE ARE TODAY

The Great Commission, issued by Christ himself, is under much scrutiny today. Yes, great strides have been made and book after book records our many successes of bringing the gospel of Jesus Christ to the lost nations of the world. We commend our missionaries who have sacrificed themselves, many times their very lives in the spread of the good news of the cross. However, let us evaluate ourselves, by looking closely at some documented and researched facts.

Robert L. Summer, in his book *"Evangelism Church on Fire,"* a compilation of lectures on evangelism given at Grand Rapids Baptist College Seminary said, *"The tremendous tragedy of the twentieth-century evangelism can be summed up in two words 'No Fire'."*

He said, *"We are sound in faith, the majority of our members live separated lives, laymen and lay women are versed in scripture, have plenty of church machinery and our programs embrace all areas of our religious life and duties".* Yet, he said, *"something is lacking: a Holy fire to ignite our constituencies and cause it to blaze, for the glory of God is missing."*

He continued, churches are growing in terms of increased membership but only eight percent of the population is in the Sunday morning worship at any one time and only two percent at night. The majority of churches make no excuses for not having a midweek prayer service any longer.

Thirty million children do not attend Sunday School or church and are untouched by gospel influence according to Daniel Fisher, a Methodist home missions authority. There are more than sixty million people in the United States living in areas not served by any church. This is forty percent of the total population.

There are sixty thousand dead and closed churches in America, and it is estimated that rural churches are dying at the rate of one thousand per year. There are ten thousand towns and villages in the United States without an open church, without religious services of any kind and thirty thousand more towns have no resident pastor.

He quoted Dr. E. J. Daniels, director of *"Christ for The World"* in what he referred to as an excellent volume, *"Techniques of Torch Bearing."* said that Dr. Daniels lamented *"We have to admit that we as modern Christians and churches are not getting the saving power of Christ into the hearts of the masses of this world."* He said he came across some startling statistics that reveal how we are failing and increasingly so. Statistics are as follows:

- In 1850 it took five Christians a year to lead a soul to Christ.

- In 1900 it took 14 Christians a year to lead a soul to Christ.

- In 1919 it took 21 Christians a year to lead a soul to Christ.

In the time of the writing of the book, it was taking 33 Christians an entire year to lead one soul to Christ.

These statistics are based on the various Christian denominations. The author felt that the true picture can even be worse than what the statistics were portraying.

The author also referred to the book *"The Romance of Evangelism"* by Roland Q. Leavell and gave these numbers.

- Twenty percent never pray
- Twenty-five percent never read their Bibles.
- Thirty percent never attend church.
- Forty percent never give to any cause.

- Fifty percent never go to Sunday School.
- Sixty percent never attend Sunday evening services.
- Seventy percent never give to missions.
- Eighty percent never go to prayer meetings.
- Ninety percent never have family worship.
- Ninety-five percent never won a soul to Christ.

We are not getting the job done he concluded.

Even when we boast of large memberships, millions are out there.

There isn't much of harvesting of souls happening in our churches today. Growth is primarily due to a rotation of church members or persons hopping from one church to another.

False predictions in the Coming of Christ

Personally, I feel that there have been too many blunders in the predictions of the coming of Christ. In fact, there should be no blunders at all since the Bible clearly states that no man knows the day nor the hour. Do we feel that we have become so knowledgeable, or are we practising super knowledge why we, on different levels, have come up with dates for the coming of Christ? I read somewhere that an atheist used the blunders of one who identified a date for the coming of Christ to further deny the existence of God. Yes, God reveals Himself and His doings in and through

His people but a declaration was made in the scriptures: *"no man knows…"* Super knowledge such as these are exactly what I see Satan displaying in the Garden of Eden.

As Eve was misled, so many have been misled. Some actually prepared themselves for the timing announced by the misled, to their disappointment and disillusionment.

In the case of Mr. Camping, this was a global stir! Folks were fooled! Preparation, I learnt was obvious in some parts and places. Some lost confidence in God and Christianity after the stipulated date had passed. False predictions can also lend themselves to deeper and darker ignorance as it relates to the second coming of Christ! He is coming again! We simply don't know of a date. Camping is not the only one who is known for false predictions.

Clergy Mishaps: Roman Catholic Priests and Child Sexual Abuse

Roman Catholic priests, according to traditional views held by the church, are forbidden to marry. This seemingly in my opinion is not supported by scripture since these men are human beings with sexual desires. I think that marriage if strong, where two people are committed to each other and to God can only serve in the best interest of the church. Those who are to be eunuchs must do so because of their convictions or according to how the Lord leads him.

In the year 2002, there was a big scandal alleging widespread child and youth sexual abuse by Roman Catholic priests. A series of books were written starting in 1990.

One article said that though there were some false accusations because of their interest in compensation, there were also some silent victims. The article said that there were some priests with homosexual or bi-sexual tendencies.

The article further stated that the child and youth sexual abuse was not just limited to Baptist but others from other denominations. The article said that an Episcopal priest, Baptist pastor and Orthodox rabbi to name a few had been involved in such.

Sylvia M. Demarest, a lawyer from Texas has been tracking accusations against priests since the mid-1990s. By 1996 she had identified eleven hundred priests who had been accused of molesting children. She predicted when the list is updated the number will be about fifteen hundred. This represents 2.5 percent of the approximately sixty thousand men who have been active priests in the United States since 1984.

The article said that two hundred Roman Catholic priests in the Philippines have been investigated for sexual misconduct and abuses over the past decades. Sexual misconduct here seems to include many offences from child abuse to rape to keeping adult mistresses.

A survey of child and youth sexual abuse within the church issued in February 2006, estimates that four percent of one hundred and ten thousand priests who served between 1950 and 2002 were abusive.

Richard Stripe, a psychotherapist and former priest has studied celibacy and sexuality in the priesthood for four decades. He has authored four books on the topic. He has twenty-five years of experience interviewing fifteen hundred priests and others. He estimates that six percent of priests abuse.

Four percent of Priests abused teens, age thirteen to seventeen and two percent abused pre-pubertal children.

Philip Jenkins is a professor of history and religious studies at Penn State University. He has written a book on the topic. He estimates about three percent of priests sexually abuse youths and children.

Personally, I think that though the percentage may seem small it was of great magnitude because it was so widespread and it involved the clergy. Also, it happened over a very long period. It certainly would have caused persons to lose faith in the church.

CHAPTER SEVEN

My God, Your God

07

> The living, the living, he shall praise thee, as I do this day: the father to the children shall make known thy truth.
>
> *Isaiah 38:19*

CHAPTER SEVEN

MY GOD, YOUR GOD

I cannot help but note and conclude that from my observation, in many cases, Christian parents do a sloppy job of drafting their children into Christianity. Compared with other religions, research shows that we retain the lowest percentage of our children. Hence we are not the fastest-growing religion.

The prophet Malachi said that God gave children godly parents so that He can have godly seeds. Children are given to godly parents so that God can inherit them. When Jacob was asked, in Genesis, *"Whose children are these?"* he answered, *"These are the children that the Lord gave to us."*

Our role as Christian parents is to lead our children to Christ and to train them in the disciplines of Christianity.

Our children are to be trained and brought up in Christianity. Our homes are training camps for the Lord. By the time our children are to leave home, they should be established and growing Christians finding their places in the service of the Lord, making valuable contributions.

A child of Christian parents should be brought to Christ at the earliest opportunity. He/she should be taught so that as he/she comes to the age of accountability at age four or five or thereafter, accepts Christ as personal Lord and Savior thus becoming a Christian and a part of the great kingdom movement of Christianity.

They should be taught that they are Christians and that they did not become Christians when their names were given, but when, after coming to the knowledge of right and wrong, made a decision for Christ, accepting Him as personal Lord and Savior of their lives.

They must be treated as Christians and training must be vigilant. They must be trained to do the things Christians do: that is, Bible reading, prayer and church fellowship. They must be exposed to missionary stories and evangelism and giving and in social ministries. Songs, hymns and other children's tunes relevant to Christianity must be taught.

Parents should note and do not be overly concerned that

their children will continue to be children:: continuing with childhood plays and pranks, such does not rob them of their Christian experience. This must be reinforced by parents, as they continue to bring the children up in the fear and admonition of the Lord.

Children love the gospel and the first place for that gospel to be taught to them is in the home. Family altars are to be raised again, Bible stories are to be read in our homes again.

Children love the gospel; it is good news to them. I'll never forget one night years ago in 1995 while doing a seminar on Child Evangelism, the Holy Spirit revealed to me that the gospel to children was like a toy. They love it, cherish it and become enchanted on receiving it. The Lord spoke into my spirit and said give a child a toy and observe the response or reaction, then take the same toy and give it to an adult. What a great impact!

Parents, the first opportunity to see our children become enchanted with the gospel is ours. It is given to us as parents.

What of our fathers, our leaders? Isaiah 38:19 reminds us again that it is to you the responsibility was given to lead these little ones. David, the father, in 2 Samuel 18:19

I inquired about his son. He asked, *"Is the young man Absalom safe?"* What about your boys and girls? Are they safe? Are they safe in Christ and secured in Christianity? Too many parents and fathers in particular *"fall down"* right here. But, why? If we are so convinced as parents that Christianity is the right way to go, why don't we lead our children there?

Jen Booth, in an article 'Parenting with an eternal perspective' said God expects us to do no less than our complete devotion to our children's souls. She said we must so direct them, that when he or she is older and sins, he or she can feel the weight of that sin and see his need for salvation.

I have often asked myself, why would John or Mary be ready to go out into the working world or off to colleges and universities and not be ready for Water Baptism? Is it because he or she has not yet been convinced or is it because he has not yet made his choice? Do we understand that he is now thrown out into the wide ocean of the world and that the strongest influence outside of God and Christianity will win?

One young man shared his story on national radio. He had gone off to college and on a particular day, there was a discussion of great theories and great men who with or by them, these theories originated. He said he listened keenly and then jumped to his feet and asked, *"Well, what about God, and what the Bible says?"* The professor looked at him and said *"Sit down, you moron. Only a moron would believe something like that."* He sat down, of course, but that day he knew he was going to stand for what he was taught and believed. It mattered not. He had the truth and nothing and nobody was going to rob him of that truth he had been taught by his parents.

Our children must be so well taught at home that they are grounded in Christianity before they leave home. When confronted with the beliefs or teachings of others and other religions, they must be able to stand and stand firm.

It is almost unbelievable but in these last and difficult days, family altars and times of devotions are few and far between. Our Christian parents are giving young children the option of attending services or not. Christian parents attend church services while leaving their children at home. It is easier to turn the television on or have them sit at the computer, never monitoring what is watched, every form of anti-God persuasion corrupts their little souls and the impact of a generation of anti-God young people is the challenge of the day.

Christian parents, could we just focus now on the lifestyles we live or our practices before the children? Sometimes they see us as hypocrites, our testimonies being different to our lifestyles and practices and hence they do not want what we have. This is a tragedy, for if perchance, they do not want what we have they will try something else.

One young girl, I read somewhere, said she understood not the deity of Christ and the efficacy of his blood but the change in her mother's life she knew and wanted. Wow!

She was completely won by what she saw in the life of the mother. Wow!

Another young girl *"breathed"* her story on her dying bed. She had been taught all the Vices by her mother. She was now on her death bed and had not yet been introduced to Christ. How awful!

It is sad, but I must report that there are those who see their Christian parents as infidels. Why? Their conversations betray them, their lives and practices also.

Children and Schools

In an article posted on www.christianparents.com, the writer said that the worst enemy of Christian children is not dope or pornography. It is the one that is fighting against the faith of their children and they do not even know how it is happening.

The writer said, *"It is happening through the schools and the mass media."*

What is happening in and through the schools daily is what is adversely affecting our children, he wrote. The lack of Christian parent awareness makes it easy for the enemy of our souls to *"bite"* our children.

The article also stated that places such as McDonalds put demonic eyed dragons to look at our children while they eat breakfast, lunch and supper. This conditions children to acceptance of evil-eyed looks and even associates it with good feelings of food and family togetherness.

The article continued that parents take their children to the school to train them.

We all know the powerful influence of the school and the teacher. We are what our teachers teach. Children, in most cases, believe their teachers in preference to their

The children are aware that the schools have been approved by the parents, therefore whatever the school says is the way things are. The school takes on an authority bigger than the parents, and when the school feeds ideas contrary to parent values, the family is in for a conflict.

One television evangelist shared a story of how his son was drafted into showbiz by his teacher. The child told the teacher, *"No, my pa does not want us in that."* But the teacher sought to involve the child by telling him nothing was wrong with it. The child went on home and told his dad what the teacher said. He told his pa that the teacher said that nothing was wrong with being involved. Down to the school, the pa went the following day, only to be told by the teacher that nothing was wrong with it. The teacher had to adjust her thinking and beliefs, at least in dealing with that particular child. Dad won and the child's confusion was over.

Christian parents should be the ones to decide and determine what happens in our schools but Christian parents are not speaking out. The fear of becoming branded and not wanting our children to be exploited or be treated as non-favourites.

The article continued that Christian parents know how to reject the enticement of dope and other vices but children do not know enough to reject ideas taught to them in public schools when those ideas sound good on the surface but are founded on ideas contrary to the Christian faith.

The writer of the article felt that humanism is now taught in our schools and that the atheist is laughing at Christians behind the mask of humanism. Humanism, as taught, is the concern for people's needs but rather than finding godly solutions, humanism suggests rational ways to solve the problems.

Humanism has penetrated all of our schools. Education systems, social clubs and other organizations have fallen prey even without realizing it. It is so subtle the writer said.

Sad to say but even religious bodies have explored these avenues. Sometimes, out of desperation, wanting to be a part of the flow of the day, the world's problems can never be solved outside of the Lord Jesus Christ. Humanism complicates things and leads to confusion and distrusts.

Wow! This blows our minds away. Drug pushers and users and gang influence are not the worst enemies of our children and parents because children and parents can see them coming and are to whatever extent or degree guarded against them. The worst enemy of children today is in the public schools where lifestyles contrary to Christianity are trained into the children. Again this is happening because parents give their authority to the schools. The children accept everything taught to them at school as from an authority higher than their parents.

The article referred to discipline within our schools and said that it was not allowed because of the philosophies of men. Again Christian parents should be the ones to decide. In Christian societies, this should be even less of a challenge.

Special Attention for The Young People

Many of our youths *"fall through"* because of a lack of support in our homes and our churches. Hence we are only retaining a very low percentage of our children to Christianity. Somewhere in my reading years ago, while preparing for a panel presentation on the generation gap, I read that only 4 percent of youths in certain American states attend church services. This is reflected in the Caribbean and many other parts of the world.

One of the reasons for this startling figure is that at this particular time in life young people feel that they are young and indispensable and that the world is to be conquered by them. They would argue, that, that is not the time for God...But also, it is noteworthy that the said statistics may be as a result of experiences, experienced in the church...

Whatever the experiences might have been, it led to resentment of the church and church people. Perhaps because of the high level of criticism and insults hurled at them regularly. Oftentimes we bring into their experiences, the negative emotions of fear, guilt, and insecurity, lowering their self- confidence, forgetting that the emotional and spiritual man are closely linked, thus raising their level of mistrust in us. Trust is a spiritual quality and when they no longer trust us as Christian adults, it is dividing.

While we must maintain the disciplines of the Christian faith, oftentimes too much attention is given to the slants they use, the clothes they wear and their hairstyles.

Every normal rational human being, though it does not always appear so, respond to love. The God kind of love of which I write covers a multitude of sin and win wars that weapons cannot. A lot of their behaviours can trigger off behaviours in us that are the opposite of love, trust and confidence. But the God kind of love, unconditional love, love in spite of, can and will bring good results.

Youth years are critical years. It is filled with excitement, great anticipation and expectations. Young people love to test things and are curious by nature. Their bodies change and develop and, with a *"conquering spirit"* they see the world ahead waiting to be conquered by them. The only problem though is that they lack the experience to steer them clear of certain ills. Guidance is critical, but guidance is only accepted or allowed where there is love.

- Love them in spite of what they look like.
- Love them in spite of what they sound like.
- Love them in spite of what they smell like.

And the love that I describe here is not just love in word but in action. It is sacrificial love, the kind that Jesus demonstrated by going to Calvary.

It is important to note that youths judge us by our actions and not just our words. They hear the words all the time. When the rubber meets the road, what they see and hear is what they interpret and determine it to be.

Love works when all else fails.

Why after years of wandering would a son or daughter return home after experiencing the chills of the cold world in which we live? It is the pull of *"love."*

We will experience the conceit of some; they will wander away. After all, the world is fallen; there will never be perfection again until after this life. Things will happen. There will always be negative experiences to confront us. Let us just do our part and love the unlovable.

The Principle of Unconditional love

The principle of unconditional love is practising a love that never fails. It has worked miracles and there are many stories of the victories it has wrought.

Principles That Should Govern Our Home

- Daily Bible reading and prayer as a family. This should include the explanation of the Scriptures. Independent or individual Bible reading must also be encouraged.

- Regular church and Sunday School attendance.

- Once the child reaches the age of accountability, he or she should be taught the implications of accepting or not accepting Christ as personal Lord and Savior.

Unity or Disunity: What's in the Best Interest of His Kingdom?

08

> For there must be also heresies among you, that they which are approved may be made manifest among you.

1 Corinthians 11:19

CHAPTER EIGHT

UNITY OR DISUNITY: WHAT'S IN THE BEST INTEREST OF HIS KINGDOM?

Church history shows many splits and schisms often because of doctrinal reasons. Splits can be very healthy. Such has led to the spread of the gospel, growth of ministries and opportunities and open doors for available workers and servants of God.

God does separate people. We see this in the times and ministries of Paul, the Apostle and other great men and women of God. Of course, Christ did not only come for peace.

He separates and divides when it is in the best interest of His kingdom. There is a time for division in the body of Christ.

I Corinthians 11:19 says for there must also be factions and divisions among you, so that those who are approved may have become evident.

For us to understand this scripture, we must understand what the love feast in Paul's day was like. The believers came together to share and to fellowship. Apparently, it was a great time for the less fortunate, they were going to eat and fellowship equally with the other believers. This was part of their worship, it was also called the agape feast. Because they were human beings, even though Christians, some serious and negative situations develop that brought about a negative impact, rather than the positive impact God intended it to be.

Cliques in the church, leading to selfishness and ill-treatment of others, such as the already less fortunate, were treated in an inferior and scornful manner, were insulted and left hungry. Paul certainly had to put some things in place and quite obviously he recognized that though they felt they were mature believers, they really had some serious deeper problems within the church that were manifesting themselves in the ill-treatment of others.

It still happens today. When there are deep problems in the church, there will be divisions. There will always be divisions when some portray themselves as superior to others or if jealousies and rivalries occur.

In the middle or dark ages after all the great work done by the apostles that include the planting of many churches, there was only the Roman Catholic church. From that church emerged the Anglican church, followed by the Methodist and Anna Baptist. All the other churches came out of these churches.

The Anglican Church needed to come out of the Roman Catholic Church.

The Roman Catholic Church had just one Bible, whatever the priest taught the people swallowed *"tooth and nail."* The doctrine taught was not entirely Biblical. God needed to reveal His truth to the searching and those who would propel it. Martin Luther, the German, was used greatly when he one day found a part of the New Testament, the book of Romans and read and realized that he, like others, were being misled. And ran with the truth he did, though it led to his excommunication and a new day in Church history. Men like John Calvin picked up the mantle and ran with it. In the 18th Century, John Wesley following in the footsteps of his dad as clergy began to speak out on the

Doctrine of Holiness. He, too, as God ordained, had the church doors closed to him. Thus, another or a new movement started. Out of one became the other while God brought his people back to what he intended them to be.

What God Intended

In John 17 Jesus prayed His high priestly prayer. His time on earth was drawing to a close and with Him were His disciples whom he loved and had shared so many of His days with. He was about to leave them and surely he would not leave them comfortless but, yes, even more importantly at this point he needed to pray that they would be United.

They were to work together for only by this they would be known as His disciples. Some Theologians have said that this is the greatest prayer prayed on earth and the greatest prayer prayed by Jesus or recorded anywhere in the Bible. He had finished his work and if these disciples and all of us who came after were going to continue the work, they would have to work together.

He knew that one of Satan's greatest arsenals would be to divide the church, in a *"divide and conquer"* style. Disunity is not of God. It is of Satan and the church has been so blind to it, thus, failing miserably in many of our initiatives and otherwise. Disunity is one of the greatest failures of Christianity.

There are too many stories of Christians who claim to be spiritual and powerful, yet not recognizing disunity as a tool of Satan and the potential it has to maim the church. Like the Christians at Corinth, we, too, are blind to the strategies of the adversary of our souls and the church.

Matta Mubarak shares some information with us as to what is happening in Sudan. The article is entitled *"What is happening in the Sudanese Churches and its adverse effects on evangelism."* Mubarak states the fact that there is an issue of disunity among the Sudanese churches is surprising when we consider the environment in which the Christian church lives in Sudan. The Christian church is not generally welcomed and her mission is often seen as something foreign to Sudan. The Christian church has survived moves against it over centuries. I pray it will survive its disunity.

Mubarak continued that the Christian community mainly comprised of tribes that were reached way back in missionary times. Missionaries and the first Christians appreciated and made the most of the religious freedoms they had but since then the results have been much less impressive. Sudanese Christian leaders have not been as successful in converting the tribes to Christianity.

There are many more tribes to be reached with the gospel of Jesus Christ, yet the Sudanese Christian leaders and churches seem content to fight and divide rather than unite, thus failing miserably in the evangelistic task of the great commission.

What a tragedy, many more tribes remain unreached in Sudan while the church is divided among itself. What a tragedy!

Mubarak, after exploring the reasons for the disunity which are not based on biblical issues but justice, asks the question, *"Where is the vision for the millions of unsaved?"*

She concluded that vision for our unsaved fellow citizens is not the main agenda for many Christians or their congregations and it should be.

As church representatives, we have lost focus. It is no longer what we have been commissioned by the founder of Christianity but rather it is all about us.

Christian disunity is destructive and its ultimate purpose is to prevent the gospel and weaken and prohibit evangelism.

Somewhere in my reading again over the years, I read about Mahatma Gandhi, whom we know was Hindu. He said he loved what he had learnt about Jesus. He was impressed but when he looked at the followers he did not see what he read of Jesus. He asked, *"Are these Christians?"* Are these the people who are the followers of the Christ he had read about?

Division in the church is undoubtedly one of Satan's best-launched missiles against the church. Most certainly it has weakened the church and many of the unsaved have become disgusted and uninterested. It is said that

Christianity is the only army that fights against itself. This is not seen in other religions. Other religions are purposeful, hence, though Christianity is the largest religion it is not the fastest growing.

I have witnessed many times in denominational and interdenominational settings the bite of disunity. I sat down in an interdenominational meeting of the clergy in my own country having recently returned. The atmosphere seemed to be one of peace and harmony. We were ministered to by a foreign minister whom I thought did a superb job.

As the speaker closed his presentation of rich truths from the Word in support of Christian unity, someone from among us rose and negated everything the speaker had said. He saw no possibility for Christian unity or unity of the clergy on the island. We were bombarded with the rightness of one theological nuance over another. I am not quite sure why but that experience plus my experience within and without denominational walls has certainly created some awareness the Christian unity is not achieved easily.

I mentioned earlier that a lot of the dividing walls in Christianity are because of the doctrines to which the various church groups hold. In a blog by Cody Kimmel, *"Shouts from the wilderness"* the writer, on the matter of Christian unity said that the disunity was because some considered themselves to be right and others wrong. Some are determined to prove themselves right. He said that being right is wrong when:

1. It is more important than the person. He likened this to a marriage, where a couple argues and both wants to be right. Both persons lose and nobody wins, the writer said. If being right means destroying someone else leaving another broken and as an outcast, it is wrong the author wrote.
2. It is motivated by pride. He addresses a concern for the attitude that one displays in trying to prove that he is right. It's his pride.
3. When it divides the spirit. Here the writer referred to 1 Corinthians 3: 16-17. Paul he said was warning The Corinthian church about dividing the church over arguments because God's spirit is one and cannot be divided. He continued that unity to God is no small matter and that nowhere in the Word God said he wanted the church to be right.

He concluded that his prayer was that if we disagree we would do so in a way that promotes and deepens the unity amongst believers.

Unity is significant to God and it is of great significance in his kingdom. We saw it demonstrated many times through victories in the armies of God. The walls of Jericho tumbled as the people of God marched together, shouted with one voice, following God's orders.

Likewise, David defeated the Philistines, the Amalekites and other strong armies of his day because his army was united.

In 2 Samuel, though living in their territory, the leader of the Philistine army did not allow David to fight for or with the Philistine army, lest there be division in the camp. They knew first hand that though David was an Israelite he was hated and targeted by the then king of Israel, Saul, against whom they fought. They could not risk it anyhow.

This might be the opportunity to win the king's favour they said. So as we say prevention is better than cure and with that understanding they did what they had to do. They secured a united army, the best option for guaranteed success.

Genesis 11 teaches us the value of unity. Though not led by the spirit of God they succeeded on the God-given principle of unity. A people of one mind tongue and purpose envisioning the task and accomplishing it. They were purposeful and they communicated with each other: *"Come let us…,"* they said.

CARM, Christian Apologetics and Research Ministry in an article entitled *"The Need For Unity in the Church"* said that one of the signs of apostasy, which is a falling away from the truth, in the church is the bickering and disunity among Christians.

Many people have been turned away from the church because of this situation. This they have witnessed in the world, and have come in search and hope of something different. Many tell themselves that they can do without such and as a result have turned away.

CARM in the same article said also that an individual or church group is denying clear Scripture and remain unrepentant after being admonished, then it is time to break fellowship with that group. The article made reference to the case with the Metropolitan community church denomination which openly advocates the support of homosexuality. Also, the evangelical Lutheran church is at risk of apostasy by entertaining the idea of accepting homosexual relationships in the church as is always the case with the united church of Christ.

The writer continued, *"The United Church of Christ, sets up a $500,000 scholarship fund for gay and lesbians seminarians and urged wider acceptance of homosexuals by other denominations (United Church makes gay scholarship, Cleveland, June 16, 2000, AP online via COMPTEX) or the supreme court of the United Methodist Church was asked Thursday to reconsider the denominations ban on gay clergy. (Church court of United Methodist asked to decide on gay clergy ban, NASHVILLE, TENNESSEE, October 2001, AP word_stream VIA COMPTEX)"*

The article continued that church groups such as these are in open rebellion against God and his word and it is Biblical not to fellowship with them.

CHAPTER NINE

What Happened in China and Japan?

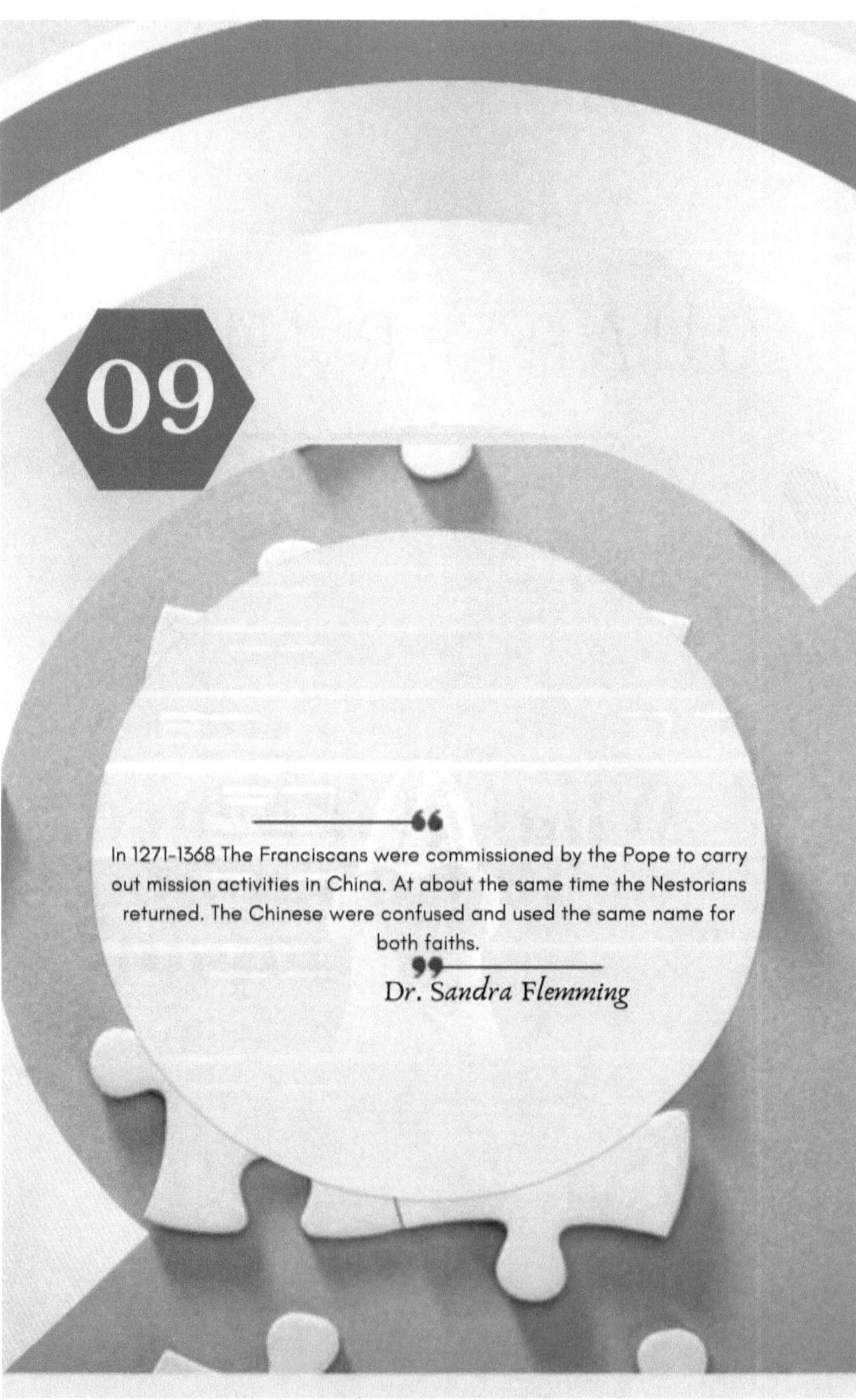

09

> In 1271-1368 The Franciscans were commissioned by the Pope to carry out mission activities in China. At about the same time the Nestorians returned. The Chinese were confused and used the same name for both faiths.
>
> Dr. Sandra Flemming

CHAPTER NINE

WHAT HAPPENED IN CHINA AND JAPAN?

Having read of the two major incidents that occurred in China and Japan and the current statistical report as far as the widespread sects and practices compared with the very low percentage of Christians there, I think that something of these two large nations should be included in this book.

Failed Missions in China

In AD 635 during the Tang dynasty, a Mission from the church in the East, who cut off from the main church due to political tension between the Roman and Persian Empires known as Nestorian declared heretical in AD 431, failed. Failure was due to the adoption of Anti- religious measures and practices in AD 845.

In 1271-1368 The Franciscans were commissioned by the Pope to carry out mission activities in China. At about the same time the Nestorians returned. The Chinese were confused and used the same name for both faiths. The mission failed.

In 1368-1644. These were the Jesuit missionaries, who eventually accommodated the traditional Chinese practice of ancestral worship. The Pope condemned it.

Another wave of failed missions occurred between the years 1644-1911. Protestant churches entered in 1807. This was stepped up considerably after the first opium war in 1842. Christian missionaries and their schools went in the nineteenth and twentieth centuries. These missions were unsuccessful.

These are reasons Christianity failed to substitute itself for the religious and philosophical traditions of the Chinese people (written by missionaries).

The early Roman Catholic missionaries were instructed not to seek for any reason to persuade people to change their customs as long as they were not openly contrary to the religion or morality.

David Paton, an Anglican missionary, wrote that the nations have their own life and culture but it must be penetrated with the gospel. He further stated that the missionary debacle especially obvious in the years since the rise of communism in China must be understood as the judgment of God upon Christian missions.

Professor C. P. Fitzgerald, writing as a historian traces the decline of Christianity in China to the failure of the missionaries of the mid-19th century to grasp the opportunities granted to them.

Also, another important lesson to be learnt from the failures of Christianity in China is that for Christianity to spread successfully, it must penetrate the bulk of the people. Christianity in China never penetrated the bulk of the people; it went to royalty.

The Kubla Khan and Marco Polo

There was direct contact between China and the West, under Kublai. This contact was made possible by the Mongol control of the central Asian trade routes and facilitated by the presence of efficient postal services. This was in the 13th century when large numbers of Europeans and central Asian merchants, travellers and missionaries of different orders made their way to China.

There were several direct exchanges of missions between the Pope and the Great Khan, though each with a different motive.

In 1266, Kublai entrusted the Venetian merchants and the Polo brothers, to carry a request to the Pope for 100 Christian scholars and technicians.

The Polos arrived in 1269, receiving an audience from Pope Gregory X and they set out with his blessings but no scholars.

Marco Polo had his East Asian in Rabban Sauma, a Nestorian monk born in Pecking. He crossed central Asia to the Khan courts in Mesopotamia in 1278 and was one of those whom the Mongols sent to Europe to seek Christian help against Islam.

Kublai was well known for his toleration of false religions. The Mongol rulers had been reputed for their acceptance and patronage of embracing Islam in Persia and Nestorian Christianity in Central Asia.

All religions including Nestorian Christianity received benefits such as exemption from taxes, land rights and economic privileges. However, Buddhism was made the state religion.

Missionary experience in Bali.

Covarrubias elaborates on the history of missionary activity in Bali.

All efforts during the past century to Christianize Bali has failed. The story of Nicodemus goes like this. He was the first convert. He was a servant and the pupil of the first missionary who came to Bali. After some years, he was baptized. Time passed and there were no more converts. The missionary began to pressure Nicodemus into baptizing others.

The article said that Nicodemus was already mentally tortured because he had been expelled by his community because they claimed that he was morally dead. Nicodemus not being able to stand the pressure any longer killed his master, renounced his faith and delivered himself to be executed according to Balinese law. The scandal aroused in Holland brought about a regulation discouraging missionary activity in Bali.

Later on from 1891, at several different times, permits were given to missionaries to enter Bali. In 1930 again permits were given to enter. The missionaries began working among the lower classes of the Balinese.

They took advantage of the economic crisis that was making itself felt in Bali by giving the idea that a change of faith would release them from all financial obligations to the community. They were told that all they had to do was to pronounce the formula: saga Perjaja Jesoes Kristos. I believe in Jesus Christ. If the man using the formula was the head of the household, the missionaries claimed every member of the family as Christians and soon they could boast about three hundred converts.

Soon the new Christians discovered that they had been misled. Things were not happening as the missionary said. They had to pay taxes like everybody else. They were boycotted and were rejects of their community. There were many conflicts involving the media also. Their community discussed banishment and declared them dead.

Village heads succeeded in bringing back many of them to their old religion.

Christianity In Japan.

Christianity in Japan today is among the minority religions. Less than one percent of the nation's population is Christian.

Reasons why Christianity is not popular in Japan include:

1. The history of Christianity in Japan is very bloody. Organized religion and war have a historical habit of going hand in hand. Also, lots of blood was shed otherwise. Though there has been freedom of

religion for more than 100 years, Christianity has failed to take root as it should.

2. Aura Catholic church in Nagasaki built in 1864, at the very end of the Tokugawa Period was exclusively built for foreigners to worship in. It later became a major tourist attraction for Japanese and foreign visitors to Nagasaki.

3. History also records that there are several Christian churches there especially in the Molomachi district but they all are built within a stone's throw of each other. Sure they have their own parishioners but perhaps working and strategizing may have been more productive for the religion and God's kingdom.

4. Though there are significant Christian churches like the shrines representing other religions, they are tourist attractions and destinations rather than places of Christian worship, though they are still used for such purposes.

5. The presence of Christian schools and universities are very minor compared to other such facilities. Though Japanese students attend, it is not a sign of interest in the religion but to do a particular course offered or because they were unable to secure a place at a preferred university. The role of the Japanese in school activities is very minor.

Prior History

Francis Xavier, a founding member of the Jesuit order, arrived in Kagoshima, on the southern island of Kyushu in 1549. His great ambition was to Christianize Japan. He established a mission in Kagoshima and baptized about 100 people, but he died in 1552. By 1559, largely assisted by the arrival of the Portuguese in Japan (Nagasaki), there were about one hundred thousand Christians, most of them in Kyushu. Six regional Lords had been converted.

At first, Toyotomi Hideyoshi didn't take their new religion seriously. He was more in trade with the Portuguese, who had introduced guns to Japan, with which his predecessor, Nobunago had firmly established his power.

When Hideyoshi suspected that the foreign missions were influencing the Japanese politically, he banned Christianity. This was in 1587. His edict was not initially enforced, but in 1587, he rounded up twenty-six Japanese and foreign Christians and had them crucified. He died one year later.

Christians thought this was the end of their persecution but the second Tokugawa issued directives in 1612 restricting Christianity otherwise, and then in 1614 banned it nationwide.

The persecution of Christians intensified which resulted in many killings.

Today there are about 1.7 million Christians in Japan. There are about one point two million Protestants and half a million Catholics.

They make up 1.5 percent of the population. Though Christianity found a following among a small, highly-educated minority, it never caught on with the masses.

Christian denominations represented there include Roman Catholic, Protestantism and Orthodox Christianity. These are divided into very small groups. The already small percentage of Christians is divided among the denominations. Seventy percent of the church has an average attendance of less than thirty Christmas is still not recognized as a religious holiday but a secular holiday.

Other Observations

One evangelist who has experienced great miracles in crusades in foreign lands spoke of his experience in Japan. He said that there has been much skepticism and doubt on the part of church leaders. They do not see the possibility of mass evangelism in Japan.

Their concern has been that there is a lot of healing cults there and that the Japanese can only be reached on intellectual and academic levels.

Although many efforts have been made to establish Christianity, they have failed, He further said, that his ministry experience is that evangelistic breakthrough there is like anywhere else; Cuba, Jamaica, Puerto Rico or Haiti.

Quite obviously, as we relate to the facts presented, we must conclude that it was the failed attempts and missions and the misrepresentations of Christianity that resulted in China and Japan being what they are today and what they have been known for in yesteryears. Paganism, Barbarianism, idol-worshipping and a culture that does not know Jehovah God.

Christianity is on the rise today, it is believed that Japan now has six percent Christians and China now has about twelve percent. These are the highest quoted figures reported by researchers. The progress is at an alarming high considering for centuries, it was one percent that was reported during this period and even now Christians have had to suffer for the faith. Even though there is much progress, there is still much and new tactics to persecution and restrictions to Baptism and seminary Education.

Recognition is given to Taylor. He among others established a successful mission in China in the 1800s. Nora Lam is a sparkling example of a Christian who suffered terrible persecution but yet accomplished greatly to the expansion of God's kingdom there. T.L Osborne, Marilyn Hickey and others of our century are redeeming the time. They are chipping away at the old block and are seeing tremendous results.

It was a bloody path to present-day China and Japan and one cannot help but wonder, what difference there might have been if the early calls were heeded and the attempts to establish Christianity not failed.

CHAPTER TEN

Christianity Compared With Other World Religions

10

I must work the works of Him, who sent me while its day for the night cometh when no man shall

John 9:4

CHAPTER TEN

CHRISTIANITY COMPARED WITH OTHER WORLD RELIGIONS

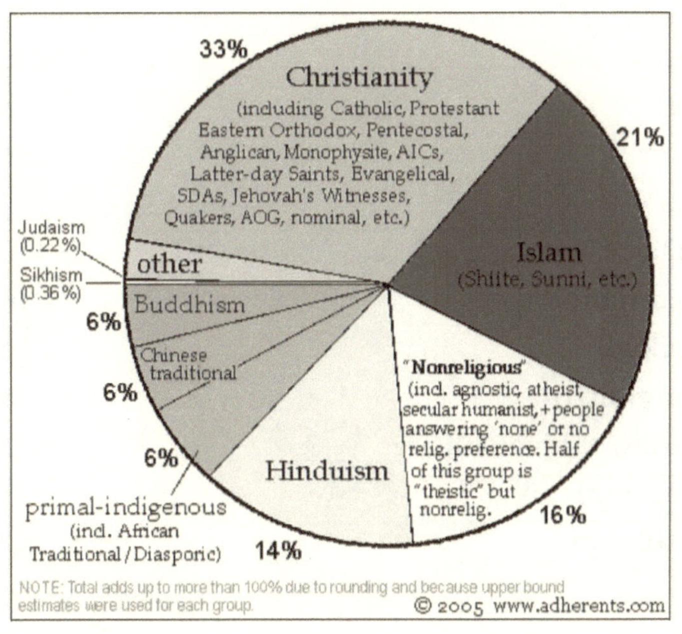

This chart reflects major world religions ranked by adherents.

Another source listed in the references gives the following information.

Christianity	2.1 billion
Islam	1 billion
Secular/non-religious/agnostic /atheist	1.1 billion
Hinduism	900 million
Chinese traditional religion	394 million
Buddhism	376 million
Primal-indigenous	300 million
African traditional & Diasporic	100 million
Sikhism	23 million
Juche	19 million
Spiritism	15 million
Judaism	14 million
Bahai	7 million
Jainism	4.2 million
Shinto	4 million
Cao Dai	4 million
Zoroastrianism	2.6 million
Tesurikyo	2 million
Neopaganism	1 million
Unitarian-Universalism	800,000
Rastafarianism	600,000
Scientology	500,000

Christianity has grown from 72 million in the 1960s to 525 million in the 2000s.

Between 1991 -2001 Hinduism grew by 20 percent.

Buddhism is being recognized as the fastest-growing religion in Western societies both in terms of new converts and more so in terms of friends of Buddhism. The ratio between this religion and Christianity is 15 to 1. Growth is through conversion.

Projections for Christianity, based on research and reported in the Wall Street Journal dated April 2nd and Article by Tamara Andi, Muslim Population will nearly match Christianity by 2050. Pew research forecast shows this. According to Pew Research Centers Conrad Hackett discusses that the world's Islamic population is growing so rapidly that by 2050, the number of Muslim will nearly equal the number of Christians- possibly for the first time in history.

This is the trend globally. Studies show that in Europe, the number of Christians in Europe is expected to decrease by 100 million from the current 454 million. The article cited that as it relates to France, England and Australia Christianity will remain large but no longer make up the majority.

As Christians, we must ask ourselves serious questions. Are we as serious and as passionate about the Master's call to

'Go?' Why are other religions seeing the increase that we are not seeing? Are we aware that we have the Master with us? Have we allowed ourselves to become distracted or weak in our quest for souls?

I read a story of a fisherman who left home to go fishing. That was his purpose. That was his intention but on the way, he noted that there were some beautiful flowers along the roadside and so he picked one and then the other, he picked another one and then another one and before he realized it, the day had ended and he had not gone fishing.

Would that be us?

Every Christian has the responsibility and was commanded to e a fisher of souls.

> *"I must work the works of Him, who sent me while its day for the night cometh when no man shall"*
> **John 9:4 (KJV).**

> *"Knowing the terror of the Lord, we persuade men."*
> **2 Corinthians 5:11(KJV)**

> *"Follow me and I will make you fishers of Men."*
> **Matthew 4:19 (KJV)**

CHAPTER ELEVEN

What Others Say

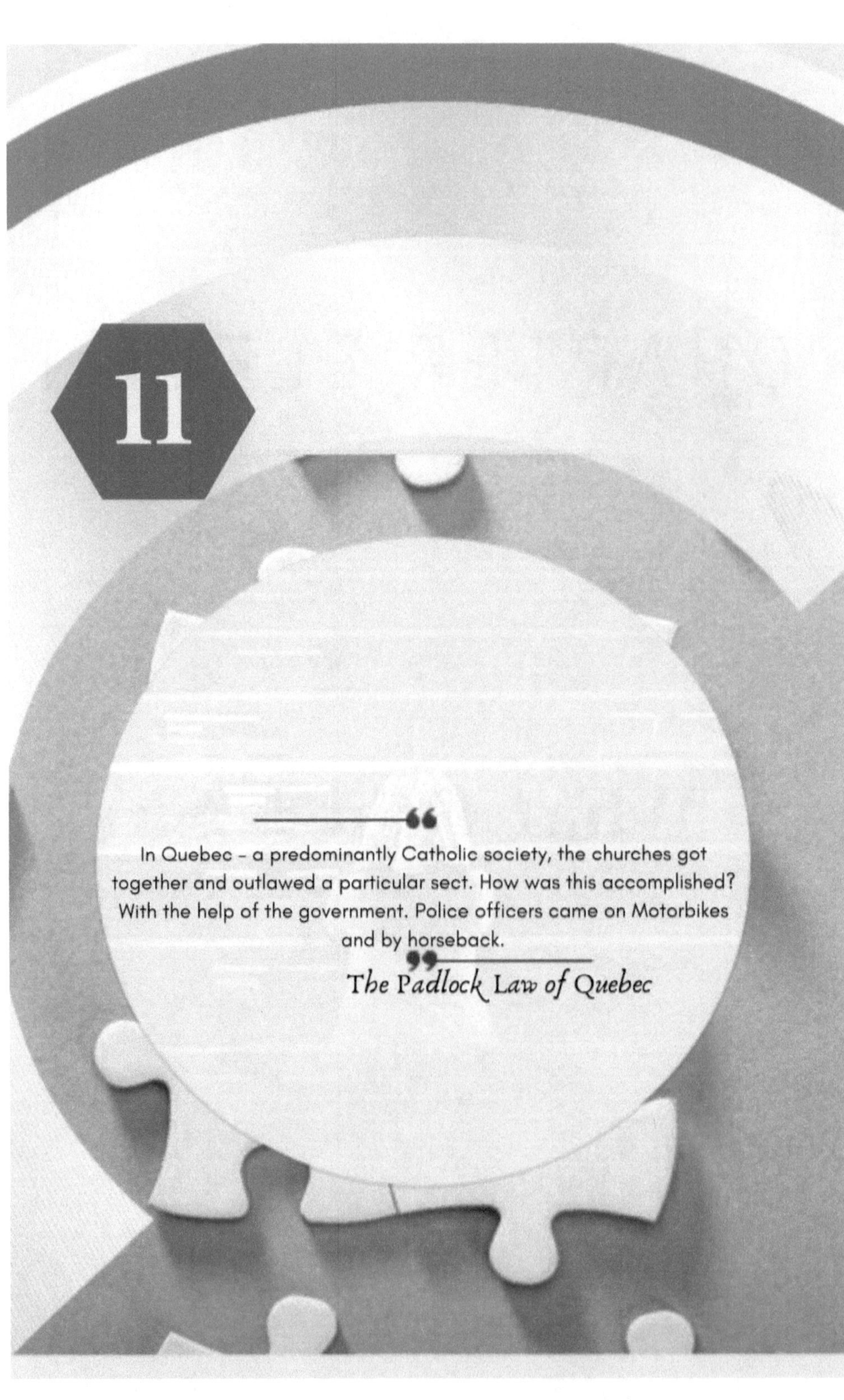

11

In Quebec – a predominantly Catholic society, the churches got together and outlawed a particular sect. How was this accomplished? With the help of the government. Police officers came on Motorbikes and by horseback.

The Padlock Law of Quebec

CHAPTER ELEVEN

WHAT OTHERS SAY

A Caribbean story resulting from an interview during my time of research. The name has been changed for the purpose of this writing and publishing.

Att is an author and a playwright. He has written several plays and books that have been given exposure in the Caribbean and beyond. He is a born again believer of Jesus Christ who currently does not worship at any particular church.

Att was brought up by his mother who took him to church every Sunday religiously. His father, though non-religious and one who never attended church, faithfully drove them there Sunday after Sunday.

Att was born in Montreal Canada but was raised in the United States. He remembers vividly and almost excitedly his early years in a church in the United States. He was pastored by one pastor who had that particular pastorate for 30 years. He remembers well the atmosphere at church, the fellowship, the pastor putting his hand on his head and blessing him. He remembers the prayers, the duets he sang and the plays in which he acted and, yes, he remembers when the pastor did not put his hand on his head that particular day but shook his hand instead. Att had become a man. It was a good remembrance and a good feeling he had of the church.

He claims that it is the church that first created opportunities for his success as a writer and as a playwright. The opportunities to sing and act, and the drama classes he attended were all at the church. He was exposed to professional training early because the church brought in professionals to train the youngsters. My association with the church, he said, led to my achievement.

He said I never saw myself as a vagabond but was lured into being saved because the church developed my talent. Actually, he said, when I went into the theatre, I felt called to that ministry.

Today, Att only visits churches; he does not support as he used to. He is not committed to any particular church. When asked why Att related the following story. He said one of the actors in one of his plays was a young man who did not always please his mother but his involvement in the play and his success at it made her proud. He was now doing something positive and the mother was really happy that her son was now achieving something.

The mom died and the young man had a request. He wanted to wear his costume or acting outfit to her funeral service. The pastor was approached but he disallowed it. Att felt that since it meant so much to the young man, it should have been allowed. He felt that this was the wrong portrayal of Christianity.

Other church experiences that have turned him off from the church include:

- He claimed that the emissaries of God who purport themselves to be leaders are not what they purport themselves to be.
- He feels too, that tele evangelists are into a lot of fraud.
- Att now does not go within a certain distance of loud sounds. Loud sounds affect him physically because of an attack of shingles years ago.
- Att believes that much more effort can be put into the young people of our churches. Exposures such

as he received as a young boy in the church should be done today.

Att further related a story of something he witnessed in Canada. It was called the Padlock Law of Quebec. He said it happened in either 1948 or 1949. In Quebec – a predominantly Catholic society, the churches got together and outlawed a particular sect. How was this accomplished? With the help of the government. Police officers came on Motorbikes and by horseback. The door was padlocked with the officers waiting outside. Speakers encouraged the people and the officers controlled people and activity with clubs. It was also referred to as Premier Duplessis.

CHAPTER TWELVE

Christianity and "The Great Commission"

> But I will tarry at Ephesus until Pentecost. For a great door and effectual is opened unto me, and there are many adversaries.
>
> *1 Corinthians 16:8-9*

CHAPTER TWELVE

CHRISTIANITY AND "THE GREAT COMMISSION"

Christianity is the world's greatest religion and it is founded on the lasting and eternal accomplishments of the Lord, Jesus Christ. As indicated in the early pages of this book, it will always stand. However, it has been proven within these pages that perhaps there were too many gross errors and tragedies of the faith.

In the words of the great teacher and master, Jesus the Christ, the harvest field is ripe and ready for harvest but labourers are needed. God is looking for conscientious committed and purposeful workers who will get the job done now.

I once read a story of a large family gathered in a single place to celebrate family. On this particular night, they retired with joy and in anticipation of another day of fun and laughter only to be awakened by the fire alarm. The children could be heard screaming as the bedroom became a blazing inferno. One father rushed into the bedroom where the children slept but it was too late.

The sad reality of this story is that the owners of the facility should have warned them that, that particular room was prone to a fire at any time; as there was not only a fireplace there but right outside the room there was a leaking gas pump. Too late, the warning had not been given...

The future of Christianity will be shaped and determined by Christians adhering to the commands of Christ, to go into all the world teaching and baptizing in the name of The Father and of The Son and of The Holy Spirit. It is quite obvious today, that our world has been shaped by our adhering to and practising of the great commission or our failure. Sad stories and lost opportunities are the highlights of the book.

Christ's acceptance of the father's will by coming to earth and sacrificing himself resulted in Christianity. Our acceptance of the mission, call and the mandate of the Master expands Christianity. Christianity in spite of the enormous growth and progress of other religion has a great future but not until we practice the mission. Paul in referring to Ephesus and the day of Pentecost said, there is a real opportunity here, for great and worthwhile work. (1 Corinthians 16:8-9).

We all have that great opportunity to practice the mission of Christ and co-mission with Him; thus bringing change to our world. How many have been left in their ignorance and darkness because we fail in this area? We have failed to grab the opportunity and have failed to go through the open doors as was reported in Japan and China.

Paul, in coming to the end, having sacrificed to the expansion of God's kingdom, said, ' I have fought a good fight, I have kept the faith and henceforth there is laid up for me a crown of righteousness and not only for me but for all the who love his appearing.'

Paul was not only referring to having lived a victorious Christian life, he was also saying that he had done what God asked him to do by expanding Christianity.

May each reader be persuaded in his or her mind to become a profitable servant of our Lord.

DID YOU ENJOY THIS BOOK?

Did you enjoy reading this book? Do you know someone that can benefit from it? Feel free to share it with them on social media.

A PRAYER FOR YOU!

Dear God,

I pray that all who read this book or even hear of this book will be challenged to walk in the divine calling upon their lives to share the GOOD NEWS of the GOSPEL of JESUS CHRIST that people and nations would be saved.

May the kingdom of darkness be shattered. May it lose its grip on our people and nations and may our world escape the perils of hell because of the doors You open for this book and the awareness it creates, in Jesus Name, Amen!

CONTACT US

Alpha and Omega Christian Centre, Nevis

Address: Westbury

Nevis

W.I

Telephone: +18697636589, +18697653148, +18696607229

Email: sandra_flem@hotmail.com

Website: www.ihcc.dk

www.jamescommeyministries.org

ABOUT THE AUTHOR

ABOUT THE AUTHOR

Dr. Sandra Flemming is the senior pastor at Alpha and Omega Christian Centre in Nevis, a church she planted 12 years ago. She is also the Dean of the Southwestern Caribbean School of Theology.

Before answering the call into full-time ministry, she trained as a registered nurse and certified midwife. Dr. Flemming spent over 20 years as a school counsellor and runs a private counselling practice.

Having learnt of many lost opportunities to reach the world for Christ during her Associate Degree days, the conference and retreat speaker is passionate about sharing her findings with the world.

Desirous that readers would be inspired to reach the world for Christ, she brings her 32-year ministry experience to the fore as she writes from the conviction that there have indeed been many failures of Christianity.

She is the winner of an OECS *"write to read"* competition.

REFERENCES

Warren Wiersbe: The bible expository commentary volume 1

Book: With Christ after The Lost by L R Scarborough B.A DD Broadman press.

http :// www.firstcenturychurchchristian.com/restoration

The story of Christian Theology by Roger Wilson

www.middleages.org.uk/middleages_religion.htm.

Free online encyclopedia Brittanica 9Th edition.

Protestant Information

Citation Information Frederick douglass.www.npc.org

www.religioustoerabc/clergy

Book :the Church On Fire By Robert Summers

www.American Catholic.org/news/clergy/sexabuse

Endnote

www.bbc.co.uk/news

www.boston.com/globe/spotlight/abuse

www.adherents.com

www.AmericanCatholic.org/news/clergy/sexscandal

Christianparents.com

http://www.colnslater.net/sudiss%2019%20matta%20mu
rabak

Blog Cody Kimmel

Carm.org

Shields.research/critics/carm/jathm

www.christendom_awake_org/pages/diancas/chinesewor
ks/polemicspdf

www.baliblog.com

www.roarfish.com2006/01christianity-in

html.JAPANSOCIETY.org

http:factsandetails.com/japan.php?itemid_592&-catid-
16&subcatid_182

The story of Christian Theology by roger Wilson

Billionblbles.org/china

Christian aggression.org

Christianity-awake

Christian post

Wall Street Journal, April 2nd 2015

Acts

Malachi

Luke

Mathew